# SHARK-INFESTED CUSTARD

## Katie Wales

Illustrated by David Farris

Piccolo Books
**A Piccolo Original**

*To Tim*

First published 1990 by Pan Books Ltd,
Cavaye Place, London SW10 9PG

9 8 7 6 5 4 3 2 1

© Katie Wales

ISBN 0 330 31430 0

Printed by Clays Ltd, St Ives plc

What does a Frenchman eat for breakfast?

Huit heures bix!

What do witches eat for breakfast?

Snap-cackle-pop!

*Cornflakes.*

**What do chiropodists eat for breakfast?**

*Scrambled eggs.*

**How do ghosts like their eggs?**

TERRIFRIED

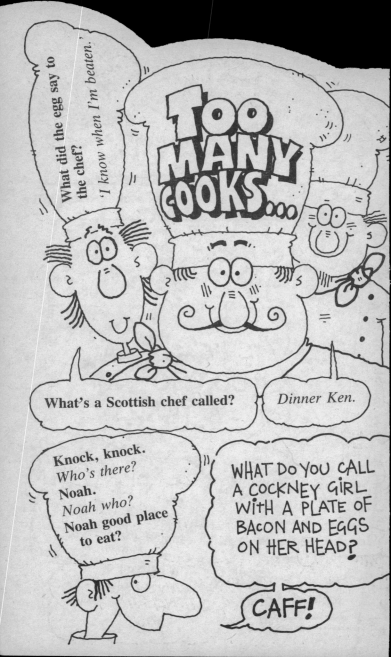

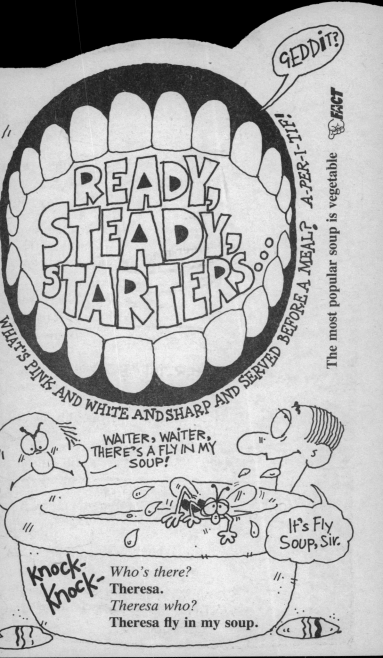

'Waiter, waiter,
there's still a fly
in my soup.'

'Waiter, waiter,
there's another
fly in my soup.'

'Waiter, waiter,
what's this fly
doing in my soup?'

'Waiter, waiter,
what's *this* fly doing
in my soup?'

'Waiter, waiter, there's a
dead fly in my soup.'

'Waiter, waiter, there's another dead fly
in my soup!'

'Waiter, waiter, there's still a dead fly
in my soup!'

'Waiter, waiter, there's a fly in
my soup.'

'Waiter, waiter, there's *still* a
fly in my soup.'

'Waiter, waiter, there's a
fly swimming in my
soup.'

'That's OK sir, it just wiped its feet on the bread roll.'

'Don't worry, I'll call the RSPCA.'

'Looks like the breast-stroke, sir.'

'Trying to get out, sir.'

'And he was so young' (sob).

'Yes sir, it's the hot water that kills them.'

'Well what do you expect for 50p: a live one?'

'Well, it's better than no meat at all.'

'They don't care what they drink, do they?'

'Throw it a pea and it'll play water-polo.'

'Waiter, waiter,
there's a fly in my soup.'

'Would you prefer it to be served
separately?'

'Waiter, waiter, there's STILL a fly in
my soup.'

'Not so loud, sir, or everyone will want one.'

'Waiter, waiter, there's another fly in
my soup.'

'Don't worry sir, the spider in your greens will
catch it.'

'Waiter, waiter, there's a fly in my soup.'
'Yes, I know sir: the chef used to be
a tailor.'

'Waiter, waiter,
there's a fly in
my soup.'

'Yes, I know sir, it's the
rotting meat that
attracts them.'

'Waiter, waiter,
this bun tastes of
soap.'

'That's right, sir – it's a bath bun.'

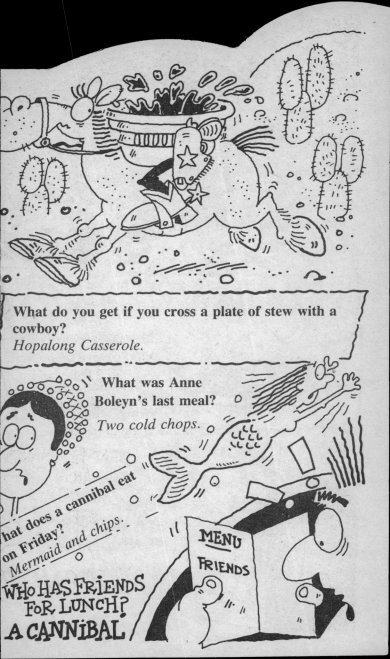

**What do you get if you cross a plate of stew with a cowboy?**
*Hopalong Casserole.*

**What was Anne Boleyn's last meal?**
*Two cold chops.*

What does a cannibal eat on Friday?
*Mermaid and chips.*

WHO HAS FRIENDS FOR LUNCH?
A CANNIBAL

MENU
FRIENDS

**What's a cannibal's favourite pie?**

*Snake and pygmy.*

**First cannibal's wife: 'I don't know what to make of my husband these days.'**
*Second cannibal's wife: 'How about a casserole?'*

WAITER, WAITER, THERE'S A TWIG IN MY SOUP!

YES SIR, WE HAVE BRANCHES EVERYWHERE.

**What birds hover over people in the desert?**
*Luncheon vultures.*

WHY IS ROAST PORK LIKE AN OLD RADIO?

THEY BOTH HAVE A LOT OF CRACKLING.

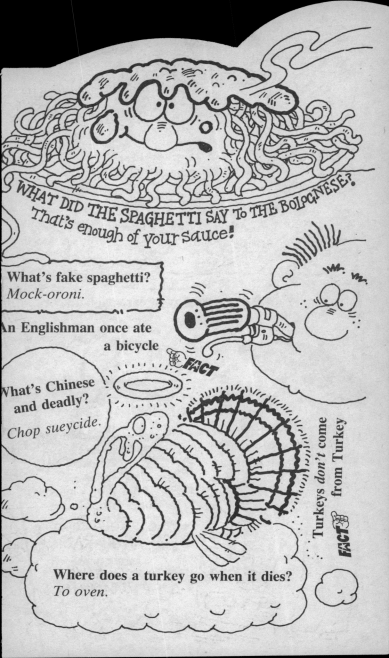

**WHAT DID THE SPAGHETTI SAY TO THE BOLOGNESE?**
That's enough of your sauce!

**What's fake spaghetti?**
*Mock-oroni.*

**An Englishman once ate a bicycle**
FACT

**What's Chinese and deadly?**
*Chop sueycide.*

Turkeys *don't* come from Turkey
FACT

**Where does a turkey go when it dies?**
*To oven.*

**What is the best way to eat spaghetti?**
*Open your mouth.*

A Frenchman ate 72 snails in under 3 minutes – and (not surprisingly!) died

A man in Yugoslavia once ate a bus

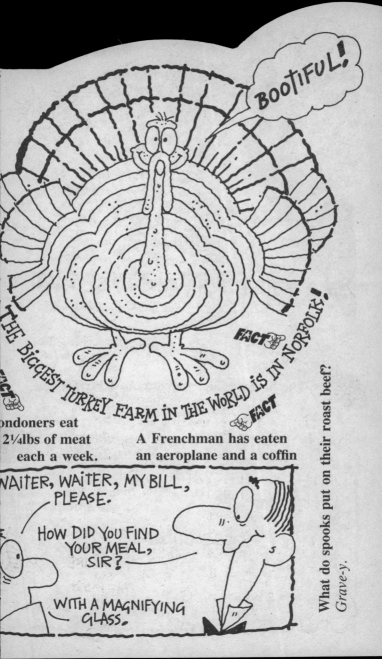

BOOTIFUL!

THE BIGGEST TURKEY FARM IN THE WORLD IS IN NORFOLK!

FACT

FACT

FACT

ondoners eat 2¼lbs of meat each a week.

A Frenchman has eaten an aeroplane and a coffin

WAITER, WAITER, MY BILL, PLEASE.

HOW DID YOU FIND YOUR MEAL, SIR?

WITH A MAGNIFYING GLASS.

What do spooks put on their roast beef?
*Grave-y.*

What's yellow and soft and goes round and round?
*A long-playing omelette.*

THE BOMBAY DUCK IS A FISH **FACT**

In Hawaii, they once had a barbeque for 15,000 people **FACT**

**FACT** THE BIGGEST DINNER DISH is ROAST CAMEL

'Waiter, waiter,
this soup tastes
funny.'

'Waiter, waiter,
there's no turtle
in this turtle
soup.'

'Waiter, waiter,
there's a hand in
my soup.'

'Waiter, waiter,
this plate is wet.'

'Waiter, waiter, you've
got your sleeve in my
soup.'

'Waiter, waiter, there's a film in
my soup.'

'Waiter, waiter, there's a earwig in
my soup.'

'Waiter, waiter, there's a cockroach
in my soup.'

'Waiter, waiter, there's a worm
in my soup.'

'Waiter, waiter, there's a rat
in my soup.'

'Waiter, waiter, there's a
bird in my soup.'

'Then laugh, sir.'

'So what: there's no horse in horseradish.'

'That's not your soup, sir, that's a finger bowl.'

'That's your soup, sir.'

'There's no arm in it, sir.'

'Have you seen it before then?'

'That's funny, it's usually a fly.'

'Yes sir, the fly's on holiday.'

'That's not a worm, sir, that's your sausage.'

'Well, you wanted something with a little body in it.'

'That's all right, sir, it's bird'snest soup.'

WHAT DO YOU CALL A RUDE SPROUT?
A FRESH VEGETABLE!

Knock Knock!

Who's there?
Beets.
Beets who?
Beets me, I just
forgot the joke.

'Doctor, doctor,
I feel like a gherkin.'

'What a pickle to
be in.'

What's green and jumps up
and down?

A sprout at a disco.

What's green and travels at 100 mph?

An MG sprout.

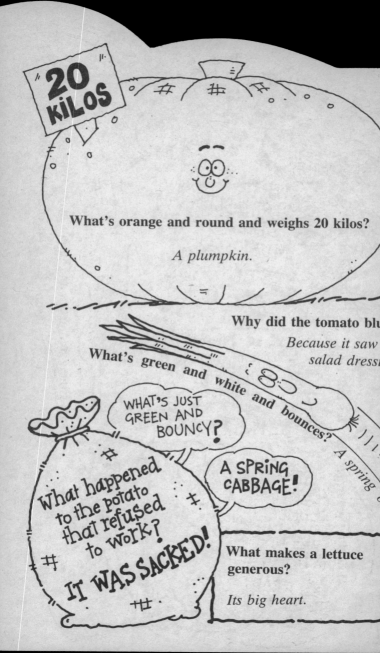

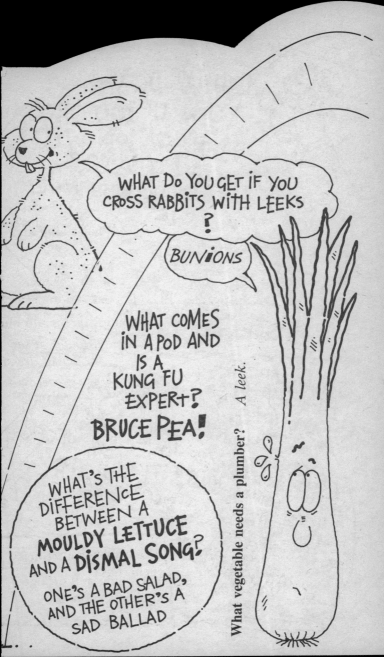

What do you call two turnips in love?     *Swedehearts.*

How would you feel if you crossed a vegetable with a fruit?

*Melon-cauli.*

*An E-type carrot.*

What did the vegetable say when it knocked on the door?

*'Lettuce in.'*

What do you call a rude King Edward on television?

*A common-tater.*

*...double-barrelled carrot.*

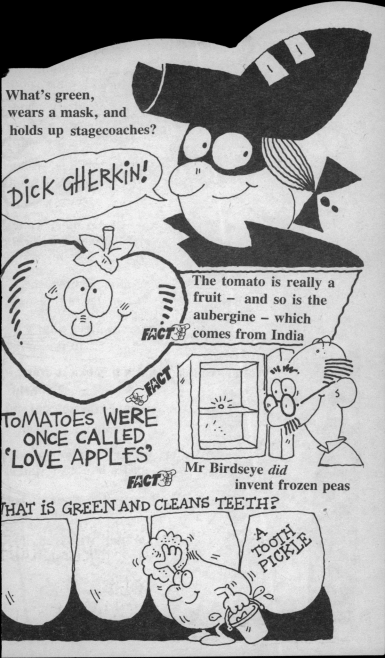

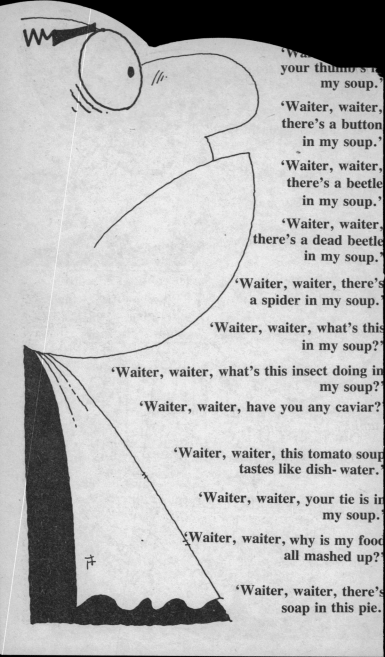

'Wa[...]
your thumb's i[...]
my soup.'

'Waiter, waiter,
there's a button
in my soup.'

'Waiter, waiter,
there's a beetle
in my soup.'

'Waiter, waiter,
there's a dead beetle
in my soup.'

'Waiter, waiter, there's
a spider in my soup.'

'Waiter, waiter, what's this
in my soup?'

'Waiter, waiter, what's this insect doing in
my soup?'

'Waiter, waiter, have you any caviar?'

'Waiter, waiter, this tomato soup
tastes like dish-water.'

'Waiter, waiter, your tie is in
my soup.'

'Waiter, waiter, why is my food
all mashed up?'

'Waiter, waiter, there's
soap in this pie.'

'That's all right sir, it's not very hot.'

'Oh thank you, sir, I've been looking for it everywhere.'

'Don't send for the manager: he's frightened of them too.'

'Yes, they aren't very good swimmers, are they?'

'That'll be 10p extra, sir.'

'I don't know, I can't tell one bug from another.'

'I think it's drowning, sir.'
'No, sir, but I could let you have some tapioca and   sunglasses.'

'Sorry, sir, I must have given you the wrong bowl – tomato soup tastes like sour milk.'

'That's OK sir, it's not shrinkable.'

'You did ask me to step on it, sir.'

'Well that's to wash it down with, sir.'

Ice cream was invented by the Chinese

**What did the man say who had jelly and custard in his ears?**

*'You'll have to speak up a bit, I'm a trifle deaf.'*

**What is sweet, covered in custard, and bad-tempered?**

*Apple grumble.*

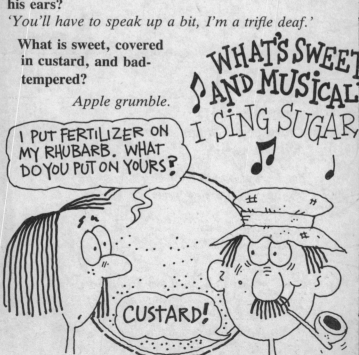

# Ring Ring

## What's fruity and wobbly and goes 'Ring Ring'?

## A JELLY-PHONE

**What's bald and wobbles?**
*Jelly Savalas.*

Knock, knock.
Who's there?
**Ice cream.**
*Ice cream who?*
**Ice cream and scream until I'm sick!**

A Christmas pudding in Australia weighed 3,064 lbs

FACT

FACT

1/6 OF BRITISH PEOPLE EAT CUSTARD ONCE A DAY

## WHAT'S STUPID AND YELLOW?

## THICK CUSTARD.

**WHAT FLIES AND WOBBLES?**

**A JELLY-COPTER**

# Knock-Knock-

Who's there?

**Aida.**

*Aida who?*

**Aida plate of prunes, and now I feel ill . . .**

**How do you make an apple puff?**

*Chase it round the kitchen.*

What's 300 metres tall, weighs 7000 tonnes, and is made of jelly and custard? *The Trifle Tower.*

Who was the trifle's favourite artist? *Bottijelli.*

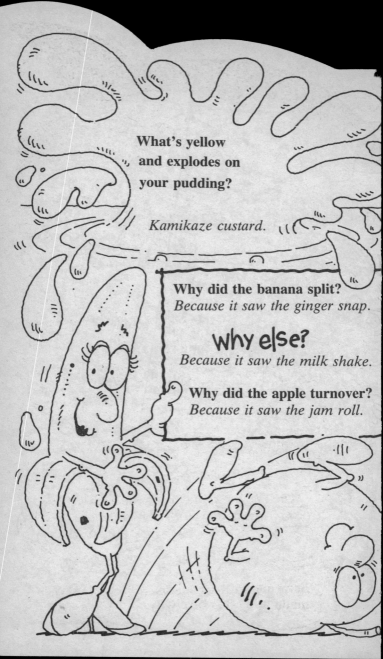

**What's yellow and explodes on your pudding?**

*Kamikaze custard.*

**Why did the banana split?**
*Because it saw the ginger snap.*

**why else?**
*Because it saw the milk shake.*

**Why did the apple turnover?**
*Because it saw the jam roll.*

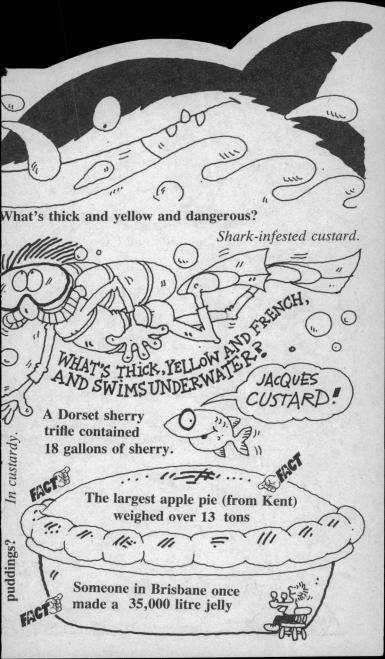

**What's thick and yellow and dangerous?**

*Shark-infested custard.*

WHAT'S THICK, YELLOW AND FRENCH, AND SWIMS UNDERWATER?

JACQUES CUSTARD!

A Dorset sherry trifle contained 18 gallons of sherry.

*In custardy.*

**FACT**   **FACT**

The largest apple pie (from Kent) weighed over 13 tons

*puddings?*

**FACT**

Someone in Brisbane once made a 35,000 litre jelly

**What's sweet, white and fluffy and has whiskers and floats?**

*A cat-a-meringue.*

WHAT'S A CAT'S FAVOURITE DESSERT?
MICE PUDDING.

**What's a pixie's favourite pudding?**

*Fairy cakes.*

THE LONGEST BANANA SPLIT IN THE WORLD WAS MORE THAN 6 KMS LONG...

FACT

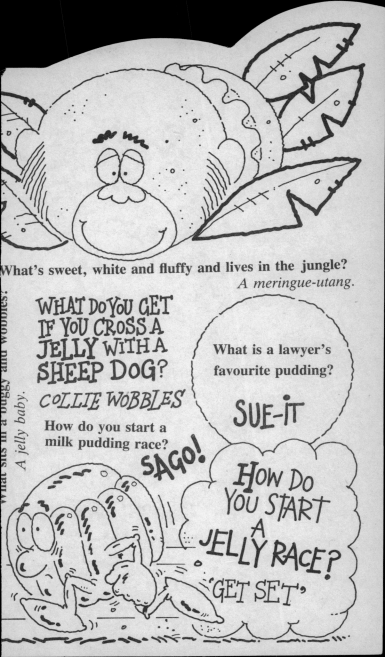

What's sweet, white and fluffy and lives in the jungle?
*A meringue-utang.*

What sits in a buggy and wobbles?
*A jelly baby.*

WHAT DO YOU GET IF YOU CROSS A JELLY WITH A SHEEP DOG?
COLLIE WOBBLES

How do you start a milk pudding race?
SAGO!

What is a lawyer's favourite pudding?
SUE-it

HOW DO YOU START A JELLY RACE?
'GET SET'

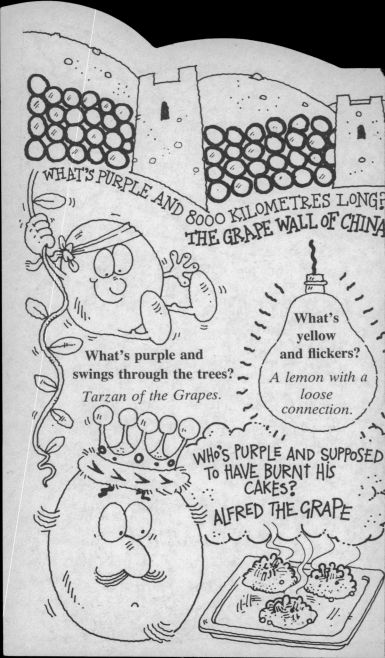

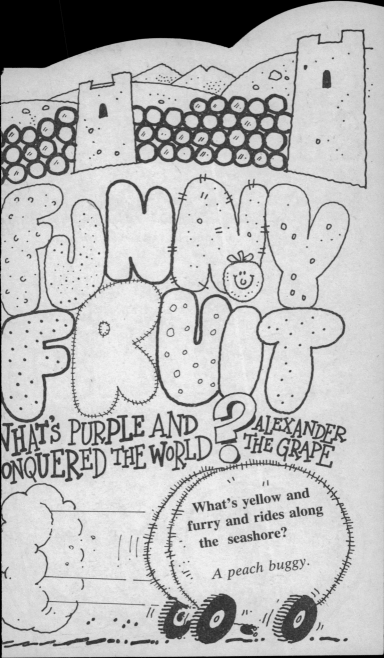

# FUNNY FRUIT

WHAT'S PURPLE AND CONQUERED THE WORLD? ALEXANDER THE GRAPE

What's yellow and furry and rides along the seashore?

A peach buggy.

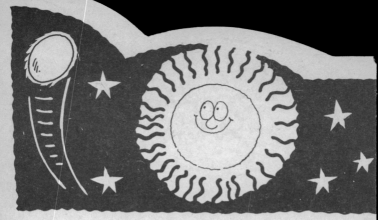

**What's purple and orbits the sun?**
*The Planet of the Grapes.*

WHAT IS PURPLE AND SURROUNDED BY SEA?

GRAPE BRITAIN

WHAT IS LONG AND YELLOW AND GOES CLICK-CLICK?

*A ball-point banana.*

FACT!

WHAT DID ONE GRAPE SAY TO THE OTHER?

YOU'RE DI-VINE'

Woody Allen called his film 'Bananas' — because there weren't any in it

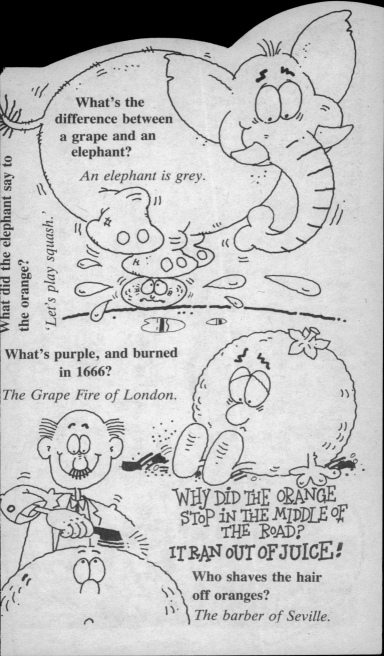

**What's the difference between a grape and an elephant?**

*An elephant is grey.*

**What did the elephant say to the orange?**

*'Let's play squash.'*

**What's purple, and burned in 1666?**

*The Grape Fire of London.*

WHY DID THE ORANGE STOP IN THE MIDDLE OF THE ROAD? IT RAN OUT OF JUICE!

**Who shaves the hair off oranges?**

*The barber of Seville.*

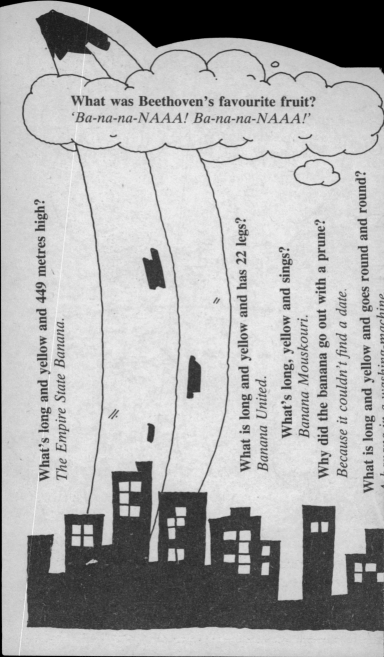

**What was Beethoven's favourite fruit?**
*'Ba-na-na-NAAA! Ba-na-na-NAAA!'*

What's long and yellow and 449 metres high?
*The Empire State Banana.*

What is long and yellow and has 22 legs?
*Banana United.*

What's long, yellow and sings?
*Banana Mouskouri.*

Why did the banana go out with a prune?
*Because it couldn't find a date.*

What is long and yellow and goes round and round?
*A banana in a washing-machine.*

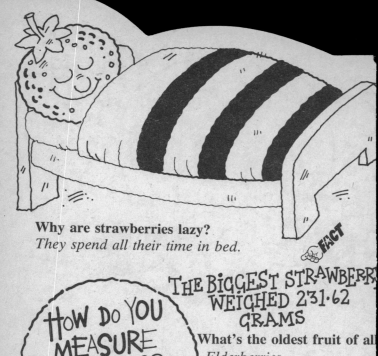

**Why are strawberries lazy?**
*They spend all their time in bed.*

FACT

THE BIGGEST STRAWBERRY
WEIGHED 231·62
GRAMS

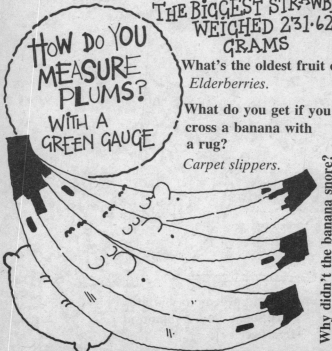

HOW DO YOU
MEASURE
PLUMS?

WITH A
GREEN GAUGE

**What's the oldest fruit of all?**
*Elderberries.*

**What do you get if you
cross a banana with
a rug?**
*Carpet slippers.*

**Why didn't the banana snore?**
*Because it was afraid to wake*

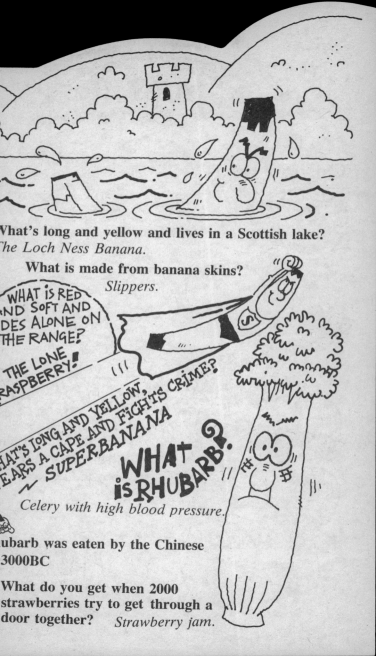

**What's long and yellow and lives in a Scottish lake?**
*The Loch Ness Banana.*

**What is made from banana skins?**
*Slippers.*

WHAT IS RED AND SOFT AND RIDES ALONE ON THE RANGE?

THE LONE RASPBERRY!

WHAT'S LONG AND YELLOW, WEARS A CAPE AND FIGHTS CRIME?
SUPERBANANA

WHAT IS RHUBARB?

*Celery with high blood pressure.*

**Rhubarb was eaten by the Chinese 3000BC**

**What do you get when 2000 strawberries try to get through a door together?** *Strawberry jam.*

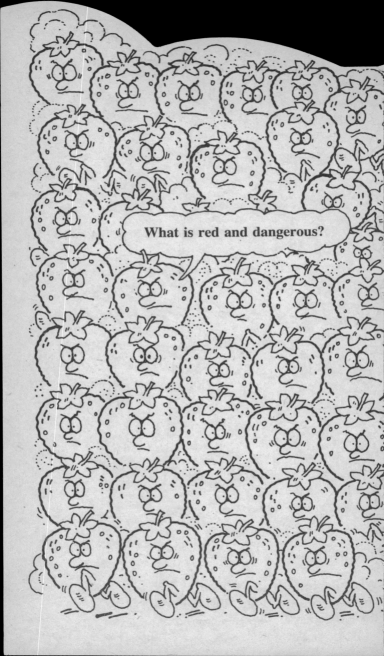

A herd of stampeding strawberries.

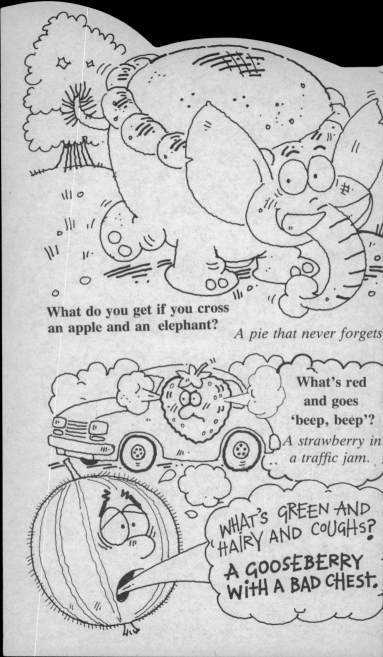

What do you get if you cross an apple with an aeroplane?

*Pie in the sky.*

WHAT'S GREEN AND HAIRY AND GOES 'HIC-HIC'?

A GOOSEBERRY WITH HICCUPS.

WHAT'S GREEN AND HAIRY AND SAYS 'PARDON'?

A POLITE GOOSEBERRY WITH HICCUPS

Who was purple and discovered America?

*Christopher Plumbus.*

Knock-knock
Who's there?
Gorilla
Gorilla who?
Gorilla cheese sandwich for me, please.

What is the Cheddar Gorge?
A large cheese sandwich.

What's white on the outside, pink in the middle, and talks a lot?
*A tongue sandwich.*

What's the best thing to put in a sandwich?
*Your teeth.*

What's yellow, brown and hairy?
*Cheese on toast dropped on the carpet.*

**What do hedgehogs eat with bread and cheese?**

*Prickled onions.*

**What's black and white and comes out of the oven spitting mad?**

*A hot cross nun.*

**What musical instrument goes with cheese?**

*A pickle-o.*

**What's white on the outside, pink on the inside, and tells jokes?**

*A corny beef sandwich*

**What's the difference between an elephant and a biscuit?**

*You can't dunk an elephant in your tea.*

What made the biscuit box?

It saw the rum punch.

What do you get if you cross a jar of jam with an elephant?

*Sandwiches that never forget.*

What do vampires eat with bread and cheese? Pickled organs

What are white on the outside, brown on the inside, and sneak around the kitchen? *Mince spies.*

WAITER, WAITER, I'VE FOUND A MAGGOT IN MY SALAD!

THAT'S BETTER THAN FINDING HALF A MAGGOT, SIR.

What do you get if you pour boiling water down a rabbit hole? *Hot cross bunnies.*

WHAT'S CHOCOLATE ON THE OUTSIDE, PEANUT INSIDE AND SINGS HYMNS?

A SUNDAY SCHOOL TREET

What did the biscuit say when it was run over? *'Oh crumbs!'*

What did the biscuit say to the almonds? *'You're nuts and I'm crackers.'*

Why do idiots eat water biscuits? *Because they're crackers.*

Why did the biscuit cry? *Because its mother had been a wafer so long.*

WHAT'S MADE OF CHOCOLATE AND FOUND ON THE SEA BED? AN OYSTER EGG

What's the difference between ice cream and a bully?
You lick one, the other licks you.

WHAT DO YOU GET IF YOU CROSS A FOOTBALL TEAM WITH ICE-CREAM?
Aston Vanilla

What's woolly, covered in chocolate, and floats round the sun?
A Mars baa.

What's soft and sweet and white and comes from Mars?
A MARTIAN MALLOW

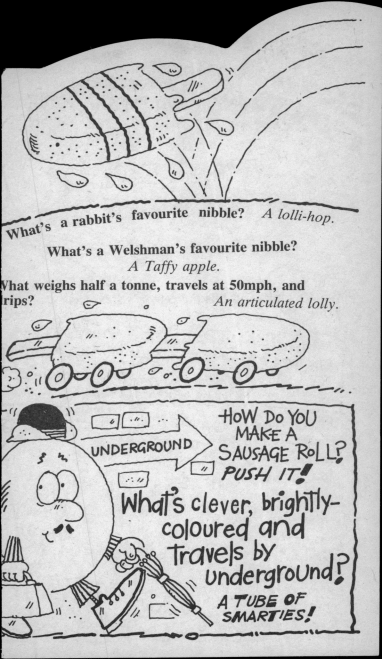

What's a rabbit's favourite nibble? *A lolli-hop.*

What's a Welshman's favourite nibble?
*A Taffy apple.*

What weighs half a tonne, travels at 50mph, and
rips? *An articulated lolly.*

HOW DO YOU MAKE A SAUSAGE ROLL? *PUSH IT!*

UNDERGROUND

What's clever, brightly-coloured and travels by underground? *A TUBE OF SMARTIES!*

THE SCOTS EAT MORE CAKES AND BUNS THAN THE ENGLISH

What's pink, and fills policemen's sandwiches? *Truncheon meat.*

What do jelly babies wear on their feet? GUMBOOTS!

What sort of sweets are good for your teeth? GUMS!

What does God have for His tea? ANGELCAKES! What's cold and comes in cans? CHILLI BEANS!

THE FRENCH EAT MORE CHEESE THAN THE DUTCH

What's red and fills policemen's sandwiches?
*Traffic jam.*

What do you get if you cross an invader with a cake?

What's yellow, and leaps from cake to cake? **ATTILA THE BUN!**
*Tarzipan.*

WHAT'S BROWN, SALTY AND TWISTY AND SINGS ROCK SONGS?
*Elvis Pretzel.*

In Britain we nibble 9 ozs of cakes and biscuits each a week **FACT**

What's the only thing to eat on a desert island?

*The sandwiches there*

What do you get if you cross an elephant with peanut butter?

*An elephant sandwich that sticks to the roof of your mouth.*

CHEWING GUM WAS INVENTED IN 1869 **FACT**

What's got 4 wheels and sizzles when it's hot?

AN OLD BANGER!

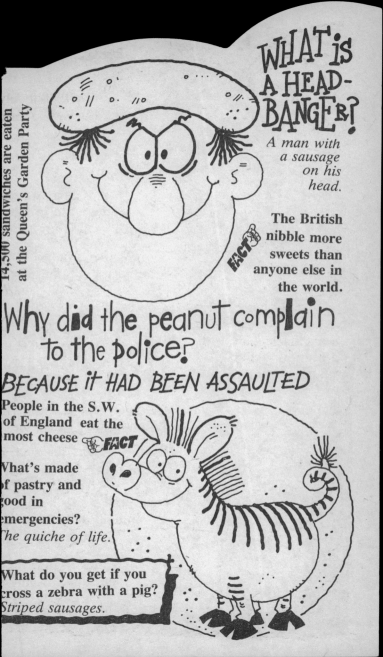

# WHAT is A HEAD-BANGER?

*A man with a sausage on his head.*

14,500 sandwiches are eaten at the Queen's Garden Party

**The British nibble more sweets than anyone else in the world.**

*FACT*

## Why did the peanut complain to the police?

### BECAUSE it HAD BEEN ASSAULTED

People in the S.W. of England eat the most cheese *FACT*

What's made of pastry and good in emergencies?
*The quiche of life.*

What do you get if you cross a zebra with a pig?
*Striped sausages.*

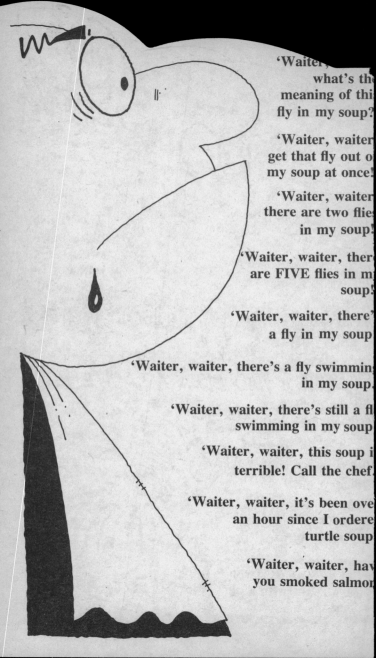

'Waiter,
      what's the
meaning of this
fly in my soup?'

'Waiter, waiter,
get that fly out of
my soup at once!'

'Waiter, waiter,
there are two flies
in my soup!'

'Waiter, waiter, there
are FIVE flies in my
soup!'

'Waiter, waiter, there's
a fly in my soup!'

'Waiter, waiter, there's a fly swimming
in my soup!'

'Waiter, waiter, there's still a fly
swimming in my soup!'

'Waiter, waiter, this soup is
terrible! Call the chef!'

'Waiter, waiter, it's been over
an hour since I ordered
turtle soup!'

'Waiter, waiter, have
you smoked salmon?'

'I don't know sir,
I can't tell fortunes.'

'Do you wish to be alone, sir?'

'This week's special offer, sir.'

'Gosh, sir, just one more and you'd
have a world record!'
'That's not a fly, sir, that's the chef.
The last customer was a witch-doctor.'

'You'll have to get it out yourself,
I can't swim.'
'Throw it a Polo mint: they make good
life-belts.'

'He won't drink it either, sir.'

'Well, sir, you know how slow turtles are.'

'No, sir, only a pipe.'

**What do you get if you cross a hamburger with a Scotsman?** *A big Mac.*

**Do you know the joke about the two-ton hamburger?** *I bet that takes some swallowing.*

**What are hot, greasy and romantic?**
*Chips that pass in the night.*

**Knock, knock.**
*Who's there?*
**Tina.**
*Tina who?*
**Tina baked beans.**

**What's doughy and 55 metres high?**
*The Leaning Tower of Pizza.*

**What did the hamburger sa** to the ketchup?
*'That's enough of your sauc*

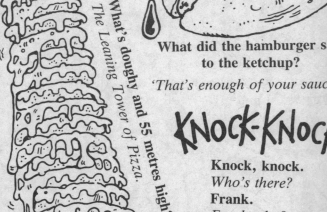

KNOCK-KNOC

**Knock, knock.**
*Who's there?*
**Frank.**
*Frank who?*
**Frankfurter sandwiches.**

POPCORN WAS INVENTED BY THE AMERICAN INDIANS

WAITER, WAITER, HOW LONG WILL MY PIZZA BE?

WE DON'T DO LONG ONES, SIR, ONLY ROUND

What's hot and greasy and makes you feel bad?
*A chip on your shoulder.*

WHERE DO CHIPS COME FROM?

GREECE

There's a man in Britain whose hobby is to disguise himself as a baked bean and eat them in the bath!

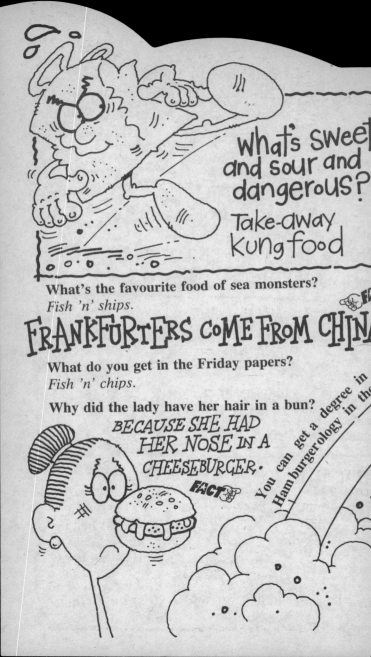

What's sweet and sour and dangerous?

Take-away kung food

**What's the favourite food of sea monsters?**
*Fish 'n' ships.*

FRANKFURTERS COME FROM CHINA

**What do you get in the Friday papers?**
*Fish 'n' chips.*

**Why did the lady have her hair in a bun?**

BECAUSE SHE HAD HER NOSE IN A CHEESEBURGER.

FACT

You can get a degree in Hamburgerology in the

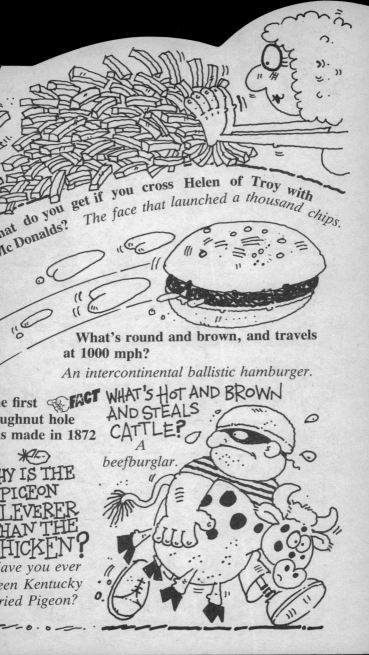

What do you get if you cross Helen of Troy with McDonalds? *The face that launched a thousand chips.*

**What's round and brown, and travels at 1000 mph?**

*An intercontinental ballistic hamburger.*

The first **FACT** doughnut hole was made in 1872

WHAT'S HOT AND BROWN AND STEALS CATTLE? *A beefburglar.*

WHY IS THE PIGEON CLEVERER THAN THE CHICKEN? *Have you ever seen Kentucky Fried Pigeon?*

**What's red and green and wears boxing gloves?**
*Fruit punch.*

# What is Dracula's favourite coffee? De-coffina

CHEERS

How do rabbits make beer?
I think they start with hops.

Did you hear about the man who fell in a barrel of beer?
HE CAME TO A BITTER END!

What's musical and holds lots of beer?
A barrel organ.

What is the kettle's favourite song?

Home, Home on the Range...

Londoners prefer tea to coffee

Why is coffee like a blunt axe?

They both have to be ground.

The largest cocktail in the world contained 300 gallons

We each drink 4 pints of milk a week on average

What's wet and comes out of a bottle at 100 mph?

An Aston Martini.

Champagne can cost £120 a bottle

the oldest wine in the world was found in a Chinese tomb — 1300 BC

**FACT**

gs at an
gricultural
ow in London
eferred Harrods
ottled water to
ames tap-water.

There is a 'secret' ingredient to **FACT** Coca-Cola that only two people know

WAITER, WAITER, THERE'S A FLY IN MY SAUCER!

OH DEAR! IT WAS HOPING TO BE PLAYING IN THE CUP!

KNOCK-KNOCK

Who's there?
Justin.
Justin who?
Justin time for a cuppa.

**FACT**

France produces more than 2,500 million bottles of mineral water a year

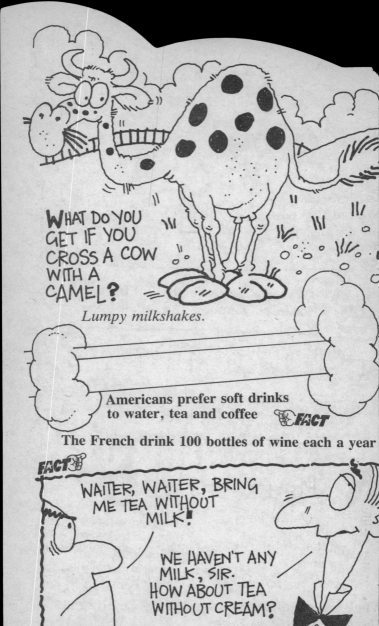

WHAT DO YOU GET IF YOU CROSS A COW WITH A CAMEL?

*Lumpy milkshakes.*

**Americans prefer soft drinks to water, tea and coffee** FACT

**The French drink 100 bottles of wine each a year** FACT

WAITER, WAITER, BRING ME TEA WITHOUT MILK!

WE HAVEN'T ANY MILK, SIR. HOW ABOUT TEA WITHOUT CREAM?

**WHAT DO YOU GET FROM NERVOUS COWS?**

*Milk shakes.*

What's the fastest drink?

*Milk – it's pasteurised before you see it!*

**WHERE IS THE DRUNKARD'S LAST RESTING PLACE?**

*On his bier.*

**KNOCK-KNOCK**

*Who's there?*
**Martini.**
*Martini who?*
**Martini hand is frozen . . .**

'water of life' **FACT**

What did the orange squash say to the slice of lemon?

**'I'M DILUTED TO MEET YOU'**

Who's locked up and wears a thermos on his head?
*The Man in the Iron Flask.*

**What's the difference between a hungry child and a greedy one?**
*One longs to eat, and the other eats too long.*

DOCTOR, DOCTOR, THIS NEW DIET MAKES ME IRRITABLE. THIS MORNING I BIT MY MOTHER'S HEAD OFF...

DON'T WORRY—THAT'S ONLY 100 CALORIES!

# FACT

Edward III once decreed that people weren't to eat more than two meals a day.

**What's a dieter's motto?**

IF AT FIRST YOU DON'T RECEDE, DIET AGAIN.

# THE MORNING AFTER

KNOCK-KNOCK

Who's there?

Stan.

Stan who?

Stan well back, I'm going to be sick . . .

THE FATTEST MAN IN THE WORLD WEIGHS OVER 476 KILOGRAMS. HE HAS A 279 CM WAIST. ☞ FACT

DOCTOR, DOCTOR, I FEEL LIKE A DOG...

GO TO BED AND I'LL CALL A VET!

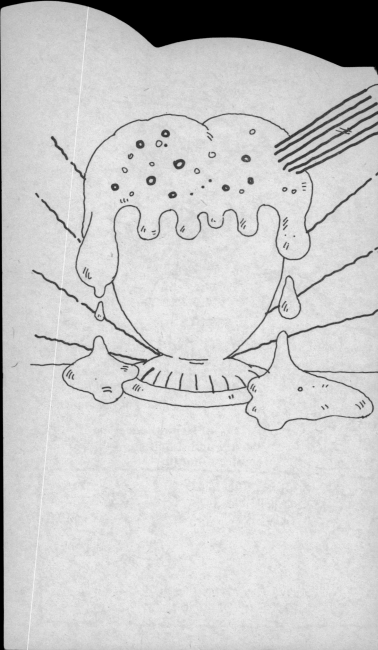